Thought

Leadership

2.0

Using Web Technologies to Position Yourself as an Expert

By Rick Hubbard

Thought Leadership 2.0

Title: Thought Leadership 2.0

Subtitle: Using Web Technologies to Position Yourself as an Expert

Author: Rick Hubbard

Description: Thought Leadership 2.0 explores a specific form of leadership. It is gaining acceptance for your innovation by using the power of the Internet. :This book provides you with constructs on how to use the Web to position yourself as an expert in your field. Thought Leadership 2.0 serves as a framework for developing your strategies to promote your innovative ideas to give you the results you want with the people who are looking for your innovations and expertise.

Keywords: Thought Leadership, Thought Leadership 2.0, Audience Analysis, Web Technologies, Niche Marketing

Published by: Rick Hubbard Consulting

Publishing website: www.theleadernextdoor.com

Cover art: Rick Hubbard

Cover art description: The design of the cover art is designed to represent the concept of "Make your light shine, so that others will see the good that you do and will praise your Father in heaven." Matt. 5:16 (CEV) Let your Thought Leadership 2.0 light shine.

DEDICATION

This book is dedicated to my parents:

Leon and Jean Hubbard

They taught me to think, to create, and to work.

CONTENTS

About this Book   i

1   What is a Thought Leader   Pg   1

2   Finding Your Audience   Pg   9

3   The Process   Pg 17

4   Core Technologies   Pg 33

5   Start   Pg 43

ABOUT THIS BOOK

"Raise your expectations.
The second you settle for less than you deserve
you will get even less than you settled for."

- Tamara Lowe on Facebook

This book is for those who want to let their lights shine. It is for those who believe they have something significant to share. It is for those who have an inner sense they are supposed to do more, have more, influence more, or make a greater difference than they are now making.

It is for those who need to extend their reach as an author, a speaker, an entrepreneur, or a marketer, by using the power of web technologies. It is for those who want to mentor, motivate, inspire, and lead others within their area of expertise, as they leave a legacy of thought and influence that will outlive themselves.

It is for those who want to develop, enhance, or maintain their reputation as experts in the organizations, institutions, and communities in which they serve. It is for those who want to stand apart from the crowd. It is for those who are willing to put in the work to do what it takes. It is also for you, if you are willing to raise the expectations you have set for yourself, and if you refuse settle for less.

THOUGHT LEADERSHIP MATTERS

Very little significant change takes place in group, corporate, or institutional settings without leadership. Thought leadership is a particular form of leadership. Managers create efficiency, but leaders create change. Thought leaders create change at an intellectual level through innovation. My favorite definition of leadership in general comes from Peter Northouse who defines leadership as "a process whereby an individual influences a group of individuals to achieve a common goal." With some adaptations, this definition can be applied to thought leadership as well. Notice the phrase, "common goal." This sets it apart from manipulation and coercion. It carries the understanding that the person being led wants what they are being led to for their own reasons.

I believe many forms of leadership take place on the Web. Every day people watch videos, post in blogs, comment in social media sites, and download products because they were influenced by someone else sharing a common goal and using web technologies to exert that influence. In fact, without utilizing web technologies, it is getting increasingly more difficult to lead in the non-digital world because the Web is so completely integrated into our cultures. If you have the ability and the Web tools you can create positive change - both online and offline. You owe it to yourself and those who need your leadership to not settle for being less than you are or less than you can be technologically. Being less doesn't serve anyone.

WHAT ARE THE BENEFITS?

Should you pursue being a thought leader? There are four benefits to being recognized as a thought leader in a field:

1.   Remuneration: Usually, the larger number of people you lead, the more money you make. Being a thought leader can help you gain trust more easily and thus secure more clients, patients, or followers. As a thought leader you may have a larger market for your products and may secure speaking engagements.

2.   Reputation: When you establish yourself as a thought leader others will come to you for advice based on reputation alone. Reputation building on the Web may help you be seen as more promotable within your organization.

3.   Relationships: Having a strong web presence that builds your reputations can help expand your relationships with others. As you help others, your network may increase through referrals or contacts with whom you can mastermind and test your ideas.

4.   Responsibility: Most of us feel a sense of social or spiritual obligation to support benevolent or charitable efforts and organizations. As a thought leader you will have the strength of your reputation to give credibility to such efforts and to influence others to join you in support of your causes.

The benefits of using web technologies to establish your position as a thought leader have to do with the very scope of the Web. Wherever your expertise is needed, you can establish yourself as a thought leader. Those who have a want and need you, will find you. Not only will they find you because of the search capability on the Web, but also because of the influence of social media such as Facebook. The Web allows you to reach not only the people you already know, but others who may be seeking your kind of expertise. When they find you, they may recommend you to others. In this way, social media creates leverage and sometimes exponential outreach as your ideas are passed on; it is networking on cyber steroids.

I hope this book provides a framework to help you understand the strategies that will help you establish your thought leadership. While it is in no means exhaustive, it will provide you with a starting point for positioning yourself as an expert. It will also point you to the core web technologies that you will need to learn or outsource. Outsourcing is less expensive than it used to be. Remember: "Raise your expectations!"

CHAPTER 1

WHAT IS A THOUGHT LEADER

"Building a business around the power of a great idea is like turning straw into gold. There's nothing more unique and powerful than creating something from nothing, plucking value from thin air, and improving the lives of others."

-Andrea J. Lee

Joel Kurtzman, a former international economist for the U.N., is credited for first using the term, "thought leader." The term referred to entities that have a reputation for innovative ideas. It is frequently used to describe the attributes of companies that are first in their field. It often refers to their marketing, technologies, products or services, their research and development, human resources development, or some other aspect of corporate life. They are recognized outside their organizations for their impact and innovation related to their businesses, their field, or society at large. Becoming a thought leader used to be a nebulous process needing outside forces to take action. Not now. Positioning yourself as a thought leader has never been more within your control than it is today. Web technologies have democratized the process and made it more affordable than it was a couple of decades ago. With the Web has come the ability to publish materials yourself. You can print-on-demand technologies or web publishing to promote them using search engine optimization (SEO) techniques to gain search engine rankings. You can also use Web 2.0 tools (social media) such as Facebook, Twitter, and YouTube to find people who are interested in them. It provides you with freedom from dependence upon the good graces of some publisher who doesn't care about you personally or wants too much control.

DEFINITION OF THOUGHT LEADERSHIP 2.0

Management creates organizational efficiency; leadership creates organizational change. Thought leadership (in general) leads through innovation birthed by individuals exceptional in their intellectual creativity, knowledge, or impact upon a chosen field. As I said earlier, Thought Leadership 2.0 is thought leadership on cyber steroids. 2.0 thought leaders use the power of web technologies to position themselves.

Many authors, consultants, speakers and researchers are thought leaders. Because of their stature, they become their own brand. This is true of Robert Kiyosaki, Paul Zane Pilzer, Seth Godin, John Maxwell, and others. Thought leaders like this are actively engaged in marketing themselves; there are some honorable reasons for doing so. For them thought leadership is more than a title. It is both a process to be entered into and a goal to be reached. Some demonstrate thought leadership in traditional ways and some through emerging technologies, i.e. Thought Leadership 2.0.

You have the potential to be a thought leader if you have something of value to contribute to those around you – something that is unique to you and innovative in some aspect. It may not be a totally new innovation; it may be a creative way of looking and thinking about something that already exists. It may be sharing your perspectives with those who suddenly "get it" because of your unique style.

Let's get a specific definition of Thought Leadership 2.0 Since we're looking at using web technologies, it's important to incorporate those technologies in our definition. Adapting the Northouse definition quoted earlier, here's the 2.0 definition of thought leadership used for this book:

Thought Leadership 2.0 is the process of an individual promoting personal expertise through web technologies to intentionally influence a group of individuals to accept an innovation in order to achieve a common goal.

Notice that:

- Thought leadership is not a trait, it is a *process*. That means it is something you can learn or develop; you are not born a thought leader.

- You have personal or *individualized expertise*. i.e. your knowledge, perspective, or methods. Together, they are your unique voice.

- *Web technology* means more than email. It refers to a set of web technologies which we will cover later in this book.

- *Intentionally* means that the leader is purposefully leading.

- *Influencing* means you are not using deceitfully manipulative methods to change the follower's minds or behavior.

- A *group of individuals* means you have followers.

- *Common goal* means the group accepts your innovation because it adds value to their lives.

Throughout this book I will use the term thought leadership to mean it in the general sense. I will use Thought Leadership 2.0 to refer to thought leadership that utilizes web technologies.

YOUR GPA

According to our definition, the thought leader has unique expertise that is a source of influence toward innovation. The unique expertise is what Jim Collins referred to as the hedgehog principle in his book, *Good to Great*. It means focusing on one thing and doing it well. Your unique expertise should be the one thing you focus on. Jim Collins gave three components; I'm going to use a variant of them. I'm going to refer to them as your G.P.A. (I'm not talking about your Grade Point Average.) Your GPA is your potential to be a thought leader and can be expressed in the following formula:

Thought Leadership Potential = Genius + Passion + Attitude

Genius is your giftedness; it's your ability to understand a problem, find a solution, or share it in a way that makes a difference to other people. It's sharing a solution that makes your followers' lives better, richer, or more enjoyable. They recognize that you are the source of that solution. The idea doesn't need to be unique to you. Your perspective may be the uniqueness. Your uniqueness may be your ability to teach it or express it the way you do. Your genius may be that you take a common idea and market it in a way that people will listen and pick up the concept, take action, or use a product.

Passion is how you feel about it. It's the intensity of emotion that drives you to perfect, to share, to persuade, or to research more. To be a thought leader you will need to feel passionate about your ideas. Napoleon Hill observed that "desire is the beginning of all achievement." It's easier to build and maintain momentum with passion. Genius will provide the intellectual engine, but passion is the fuel that will give it power. It is difficult to become a thought leader if you don't feel passionate about the ideas you're sharing. You may not need to express your passion in an overtly emotional way, but passion has to be at the core of your leadership.

ATITUDE TOWARD PERSONAL DEVELOPMENT

Attitude is your commitment to your ideas – your commitment to better yourself, driven by your passion and your genius. Attitude is both the mental framework and the resulting actions. Sometimes it means facing a truth about ourselves that we are lacking in some underlying relational skill. Attitude is your commitment to grow personally to communicate well with the people that will follow your ideas. In a sense commitment means becoming a servant to your message (expertise) so you can serve your future followers.

Personal growth may require changing your attitude about yourself. Many people have a wrong sense of humility. Being a thought leader and working to establish your thought leadership is not egotism. If you have been blessed with a genius and passion to serve, there is nothing self-aggrandizing about sharing your genius with those who may be looking for it. The most humble religious leaders actively make disciples; they say, "follow me." Your attitude should be one of willingness to serve those who wait for your unique expertise. You do not serve anyone by making yourself to be less than you are in the name of humility. Attitude is your posture toward personal change and self-development. Your attitude demonstrates the value you place on what you offer.

ATTITUDE IS INTENTIONALITY

Intentionality is a special kind of attitude. I separate it here to differentiate it from the attitude that you may have toward your genius, your passion, self-development or worthiness. The mental attitude behind intentionality is a strong work ethic; it just does the work. Intentionality is a positive attitude toward the work processes. It is your commitment to doing the work so people can benefit from your ideas. Sometime the process is tedious and requires self-denial. It doesn't happen by accident. Leaders operate with great intentionality at one or more levels. There are no lazy thought leaders.

Thought leaders have the will-power to persevere, to eliminate competing media, and to create and refine their messages. It means eliminating media that may distract so you have time to create media that contains your message. It will mean commitment to learning enough about web technologies to determine which technologies are best to accomplish your goals.

If your ideas will be of value to others, then it's worth serving the message you will share. Serving your message means refining it until it is the quality that represents you and your innovation well. Your core passion has to be sufficient to drive you to be intentional about tasks that produce quality when you're not passionate about doing them. Intentionality is following through when the passions temporarily ebb and the intellect is no longer fascinated by the newness of your innovation. Intentionality will cause you to set goals and achieve them.

There are obviously some people who weren't intentional about becoming thought leaders. They may have been motivated to excel in their chosen fields, or were driven by their passion and genius to make the commitment to being an expert even without recognition. However, you can take a hand in the process of becoming a thought leader. You can be the captain of your journey.

How do you do that? Sometimes you begin with the end in mind. You may need find a hero who has done it, and then reverse engineer the process. Figure out what the thought leader has done, and then recreate that process for yourself. Success leaves clues. Follow those clues. Study the psyche of thought leaders; study the strategies of 2.0 thought leaders. Define what you want to do. Learn what others did to succeed, and then do what they did.

You may have already achieved a position of leadership. If you are intentional about doing the work and learning some new skills, you can leverage that into Thought Leadership 2.0. There is no single path to

Thought Leadership 2.0. Realize that all paths to Thought Leadership 2.0 are paved with strong intentionality.

Realize that you can intentionally (work to) change your GPA. You can educate yourself to change your genius. As you do that, you may become passionate about a new topic or product, and changing your attitude is a matter of personal will power and focus. This is an important concept because the area of expertise you think you will start in may need to be refined; you may need a subset of it. You may need to develop new depth or breadth to your genius to be a thought leader.

As you finish this chapter, why not make a list of topics that you think could become a genius for you to focus on? What are subtopics related to them? Which ones are you the most passionate about? Why not rate them according to your commitment and intentionality toward them?. I've placed a GPA worksheet to help you with this process. It is located under *Thought Leadership Resources* available at www.theleadernextdoor.com.

Rick Hubbard

CHAPTER 2

FINDING YOUR AUDIENCE

"Get ready for me love,'cause I'm a "comer"
I simply gotta march, my heart's a drummer
Nobody, no, nobody, is gonna rain on my parade!"

From the musical, "Funny Girl"

I'm always amused by the somewhat philosophical question: "If a tree falls in the forest and no one is present, does it make any sound?" What if the question was re-phrased: "If a thought leader has no thought followers, does thought leadership really exist?" I'm not sure about the answer to the falling tree question, but based upon our definition of leadership, I can say that without thought followers, there are no thought leaders. One of the primary requirements for thought leadership is that it be recognized by others. Without a following, potential thought leaders are simply people with good, or maybe even brilliant ideas, but that is all; they are not thought leaders. It's like having a Facebook account with no friends in it. To be a thought leader there must a group of individuals who become the thought followers.

As a potential thought leader you have a potential parade of followers. I don't mean potential parade because they don't exist. I mean potential in the sense of potential energy. Wikipedia defines potential energy this way: "potential energy is the energy stored in a body or in a system due to its position in a force field or due to its configuration." I remember from physics class that energy can be converted from one form to another. When two sticks are rubbed together to create a fire, you have the energy of movement (friction) that is converted into heat. You know what your potential is from your GPA covered in Chapter 1. When you connect with an audience that matches your GPA, together you have a system with potential energy capable of being converted to thought leadership.

The issue becomes: "How do you recognize your potential parade of followers?" Let's look at some of the factors you could use to identify who your potential followers might be and where you might find them.

SPEAK THE LANGUAGE

One way that you will recognize your potential followers is their language; they will speak the same language you do. *Ni hau. Hola. Shalom.* They all communicate hello in Mandarin, Spanish, and Hebrew respectively. People who speak those languages would recognize the words immediately. Nearly all fields of study, disciplines, institutions, or systems have their own language. Golfers speak "Golf-ese," and engineers speak in "Engineer-ish." Next time you're at an event where strangers are socializing with each other, notice the animation (release of potential energy) that occurs when an individual connects with someone in the same profession, hobby, or sport, or from the same alma mater. Your common language creates the possibility of relationship development.

Have you ever been in a small group where there was a novice in the subject area who tries to impress experts in the group? When the novice tries to take the lead in a conversation, everyone else recognizes that the novice's lack of depth in the subject. It can make the conversation uncomfortable as the rest of the group is left to decide how to respond. Now if the novice asks questions and demonstrates a desire to learn, it becomes a different matter. Conversations will often come alive as others begin to share with the novice. Your potential followers will likely come from those who are in the novice category; they will be those who want to learn. They might also be experts in the same field who want to exchange perspectives with you.

SHARED PASSION

Another way to recognize your potential followers is shared passion about the same topics. In my position at a university I work with many faculty members. I was eating lunch with a faculty member who has a doctorate in mathematics. I asked this math professor, "What excited you in your advanced studies of mathematics?" She replied excitedly, "Slope! I'm fascinated by slope!"

I remembered a little about slope from high school and college math classes, but I don't remember it being anything that generated passion for me. It was simply about the angle line on an x/y axis. I definitely wouldn't be part of the "slope" parade. I would never have the passion or commitment make it as a thought leader or follower in the "slope" parade. I might build a website for client about it, but it's not a GPA topic for me. You will recognize potential followers because they will share your passion about your area of expertise.

SHARED MEDIA

Your potential followers probably consume the same media that you do. They read the same material and visit the same websites as you do; they would like hanging out at the same conferences as you would.

A word of caution: remember the GPA at this point. Sometimes we consume media because we're entertained by it. This doesn't mean we have genius or commitment for it. You may be fascinated and entertained by many subjects. I know I am. It's like the little boy, who when asked what he wants to be when he grows up answers, "a doctor, a cowboy, a football player, and a fireman." He may have the ability to do them all but he will need to make a passionate commitment to one.

Because we're considering Thought Leadership 2.0, we're talking about web media. If you are not currently consuming web-based media in your expertise, you'll need to engage with that media to find your thought followers. Webinars, blogs, and forums related to your topics are media on the Web where your potential parade is engaged. Consuming that media is a great analysis tool. You will find the answers to several questions by participating in the media?

- What are the issues that concern the participants?•
- Who is already considered an expert in the subject?
- What types of products are they buying in the field?
- What innovations or perspectives might be uniquely yours?
- How many are interested in the subject?

NOT TOO BIG - BUT NOT TOO SMALL

You will want to know you are reaching an audience with potential. There may be a lot of competitors, and it may be hard to get noticed if your audience is too big. In reality, your parade will probably be somewhat smaller than "everyone." Thought leaders are sometimes so passionate and committed to their ideas that they forget that not everyone is. On the other hand, it may be wasteful of your time and resources to develop yourself as a thought leader in a subject that is so narrow there are few people who share your interest in it. Many audiences are large enough that there may be subsets or specialties within them. A subset like this is often called a "niche." In marketing it is referred to as niche marketing.

At this point you should begin see a correlation between certain subgroups of the potential audience and subtopics of your GPA. For example, Kyle is a newly-graduated pharmacy student who is passionate about diabetes management. He is volunteering this summer at a camp for children with diabetes. He is passionate about the science of understanding it and will probably be committed to some kind of community involvement with the issue of diabetes. That's an example of someone who has a genius for pharmacology and is passionate about the subset that is concerned with diabetes management. That's his GPA. If his niche is diabetes management, it changes his audience. All pharmacologists may be interested in pharmacology but all of them may not be focused on diabetes management. However, there may be people with diabetes or community health organization personnel who are interested in diabetes management, but not interested in pharmacology in general. They might be a viable audience for Kyle. You want to establish yourself as a thought leader with the right subsets of both your GPA and a viable audience.

BASIC KEYWORD RESEARCH

How do you determine the potential size of your niche market? You use a process known as keyword research. Keywords are the terms that people type into search engines such as Google, Bing, or Yahoo when they want to find information on a topic. Sometimes keywords are also called search terms. Teaching the more sophisticated methods keyword research is not the purpose of this book but there are a couple of quick tools that I use to determine an idea's potential for development. I look at three things:

1. The number of pages that exist on the Web for a particular search term.

2. The type of delivery systems which are available for the information

3. The number of searches that are taking place for a keyword.

Knowing these three things provide you with insights into the audience size, the type of media they like to consume, and who other thought leaders in the subject may be.

The following procedure is a good method to begin looking at the extent of the documents given a specific topic. If the following text explanation seems a little complicated, I have placed a video under the *Thought Leadership Resources* at www.theleadernextdoor.com. Here's how it works. I will use Google as an example since it is the most visited search engine. I went to Google.com and searched for dog training. I typed in *dog training*. At the top of the search page it reads that there are 45,200,000 pages. That's too large to be a reachable niche. First let's fix that problem. The way Google works searching for dog training could give me results that include a page about training horses to let a dog ride them. As long as the word *dog* and *training* are anywhere in the webpage, it will return it them if they relevant to actually training dogs or not.

If we put *dog training* in quotation marks, then the search will only list pages where *dog* and *training* appear together in that order. Using the terms in quotation marks, yields 26,500,000 results. That's better but there will still be a lot of competition to a thought leader with that topic. Maybe I'm interested in the subtopic of crate training my dog. *"Crate Training a Dog"* gives us 2,220,000 results. I entered *"Crate Train a Puppy"* and there were 150,000 results. I entered, *"Crate Training a Jack Russell Puppy"* and it returned two results indicating that niche is too small. Do you see how using only a search engine, I could go from a category that had 45,200,000 pages down to two pages?

I want to be a 2.0 thought leader in puppy training, subtopics closer in size to the 150,000 results are the most practical area to consider. You can use this process for any keyword you want to research. As you are doing the searches, Google will likely suggest other terms that might interest you.

It is also worthwhile to analyze the first two or three pages of rankings returned by a Google search to see what kind of pages are ranked. With our phrase about crate training a puppy, the search returns: standard web pages, YouTube videos, and other delivery systems. Also look at the Google Adwords at the top and sides of the Google page. A quick perusal will show you what kind of media your niche consuming and how they are communicating online. The ads will show you what people are buying related to your niche. In the case of crate training a puppy there were ads for dog food, crates, and obedience classes.

The next thing you want to know is how many people are searching for those terms. Google has a free tool. In a search box type in : "Google Keyword Tool" and you will find their Adwords Keyword Tool. As an example, doing a search for "crate training a puppy" in the Adwords Keyword Tool shows that there are 3,600searches a month for that exact phrase. If you need help using the tool, a search for "How use the Google keyword tool" will give you all the help you need.

Look how much information we've gleaned from a few simple searches. Revisit your GPA list from Chapter 1. Think about a potential parade. What are the people in your parade like? Are they a particular gender or educational level? Do they live in a specific region? Do they have a specific need? Do they work in a particular field? Write down any questions you might like to have answered about them? Next do a little keyword research to clarify your image of who the audience might be and what exists related to your topic. Look at the media that is available on your topic.

One final thought on keyword research is to check out variations of the keyword. For example, dog training, puppy training, and train a dog are all variations on a topic. Build a business, start a business, and business start-ups are all related subtopics to the same concept. You may be surprised at which terms are the most popular. I suggest thinking about synonyms and different verb forms of the term you are searching for.

Write down your findings. Put them into a table or create a sketch of some kind to organize them. You'll be surprised at the clarity it brings you. You should now be armed with some good information to help you organize your decision making. There is an Audience Analysis Worksheet available at www.theleadernextdoor.com under *Thought Leadership Resources*.

CHAPTER 3

THE PROCESS

"If you deliberately plan on being less than you are capable of being, then I warn you that you'll be unhappy for the rest of your life."

- Abraham Maslow

Our definition of Thought Leadership 2.0 states it is a process. You will need to develop a system that supports the process. I have a degree in eLearning and Instructional Design. There is a process used by instructional designers that is a series of stages that used to design training. The process can be adapted to design your assets and systems to position yourself as a 2.0 thought leader.

The stages are:

1. Analyze
2. Design
3. Develop
4. Implement
5. Evaluate
6. Adjust and Leverage

ANALYZE

In analysis you are going to connect the following:

- Your GPA List

- Your Audience Characteristics List

- Keyword Research

At the end of the analysis stage you should be able to articulate the topic or niche in which you're going to promote yourself as a thought leader. You should also have a good idea about some of the characteristics of your potential audience and also have an idea of the kind of media you will want to develop. In Chapter 1, you made a list of topics and subtopics. You should work with this list in the analysis stage as you gather more information. What your GPA list did was take many things off the table -- things that you are not going to consider because they are outside your GPA. Knowing what to eliminate is an important skill. It's like moving from sunlight (which lights the whole landscape) to a flood light.

AUDIENCE CHARACTERISTICS

Your parade analysis should start with the most important person. The most important person you will meet on the parade is your potential first follower. Note that this person may not be an actual follower, but instead, a prototype of who your other followers are likely to be. This individual is the first person who wants your advice, your information, or your perspective because of its perceived value. It's entirely possible that your prototype may become your follower if you foster active engagement.

The first follower you get is a powerful person. The first follower is the one who turns you into a leader. Two things need to happen when you have a follower. You need to engage in honest analysis, and you need two-way communication. What perceived needs or problems exist? How urgently does the follower wish to resolve those issues? What media does the follower prefer? What ideas seem to resonate? How long might the follower remain interested? Is the follower a representative of others or an anomaly? Where can you go to engage more people like your first follower? You need to communicate with the follower. Together, you and the follower can create a community. This has the potential to double your efforts to reach a greater audience: you and the follower both reaching out to invite others to engage in the conversation and media exchange. That's why the first follower is so important.

Where will you find the prototype follower? Look within social media on the Web. This means finding blogs, Facebook groups, forums, and YouTube channels to engage in where potential followers are interacting online. Look offline. It may mean going to clubs (business or professional…not the party kind), joining an organization, or attending a conference related to your GPA.

Start with the low-hanging fruit which are the web-based options. They are also the strongest options since you'll be using the Web to establish your Thought Leadership 2.0. They are also the quickest option; in a week or two you can probably find your first follower on the Web.

One word of caution: don't label them your first follower unless they are the type of follower you are truly desire. There's no such thing as a needy thought leader. If your niche is hairstyling for weddings, an ideal type of follower might be a hairstylist or wedding planner, but probably not a young mother looking for instructions on cutting her children's hair at home.

Engage potential followers and ask lots of questions to determine their challenges, problems, and perceived needs. Search blogs, forums, and social media to see if there are others like them who have similar concerns. And then look to see if your GPA can meet solve their problems. When you have done this, modify the audience characteristics list you created in Chapter 2. Again, don't try to make it perfect. You'll refine it even more after the next step which is keyword research. If our GPA worksheet is like a flood light, our audience worksheet is like a spot light. Now let's turn it into a laser beam with keyword research.

ADDITIONAL KEYWORD RESEARCH

A few years ago I was working with an uncle on a small construction project and he gave me the admonition: "Measure twice - saw once." When proper keyword research done, it's like the joke my uncle used to say: "I cut it off twice and it's still too short." Doing careful keyword research can keep you from missing the mark later on. Keyword research will allow you to test and verify that what you researched.

Laser beams have some powerful applications. They can be used for surgery; they can be used for guidance systems; they can be used for drilling through stainless steel. Your keyword research allows you to take your niche topic, your audience characteristics, and drill down into data to test and verify that justification exists to make a commitment to developing the materials you will deliver.

It will also show you likely competitors and what they are delivering. Competitors aren't bad; competitors usually confirm that there is a market. You just need distinctive innovations.

The challenge is to find market that is small enough so that you can position yourself within it, but large enough to justify the investment. I suggest you spend a couple of hours researching your topic's keywords. There is a video under *Thought Leadership Resources* at www.theleadernextdoor.com. In it I demonstrate techniques I use for keyword or niche research. Once you've done the research, you should have a strong enough analysis to write a definition of what it is you will do as a thought leader. We'll call that definition your elevator speech.

YOUR ELEVATOR SPEECH

For the final stage of your analysis, I suggest you write an elevator speech that can be delivered in under a minute. Imagine you are in an elevator and have under a minute to explain what you do (to explain your expertise). If you wanted to lead a parade you might have a flag or sign you carry for your followers to gather around you. Your elevator speech is your flag. Writing your elevator speech will serve as a tool to bring the parts of your analysis together. For example, here is the elevator speech for my consulting business:

Hello My name is Rick

Step by step I help you move from being an entrepreneur to being a thought-leader. I mentor you in the process of standing out from your competition through developing and managing your web reputation as the expert in your chosen field.

I do this through web publishing of books, articles, videos, or other materials. I train you to do it by yourself, I do it with you, or I do it for you. I become your editor, your ghostwriter, your web video producer, or your internet publicist because "if you don't exist on the Web...you don't exist."

Do you want more readers, customers, or clients from the Web? I use an internet marketing system based upon the components Michael Dell defined as the 3 C's: Content, Commerce, and Community. It takes all three to be successful. Together you and I can increase your success step by step.

My niche, my audience, and the technology I use are obvious in my elevator speech. My audience consists of people who want to become thought leaders through publishing books, articles and videos; the web is my technology.

Take a few minutes to write an elevator speech. Remember you can also write another one for a different niche later if needed. Just get your best one down and then ask yourself: "Can I be intentional about this?" If the answer is "yes," we are ready to move on to the next part.

Using the knowledge and perspectives you gained we are going to design a web strategy to position yourself as a 2.0 thought leader.

DESIGN

How do you begin to design the comprehensive strategies you will use? I can't provide specifics here for a couple of reasons. One is that your selection should be based on your specific research. Your strategy needs to be tied to your keyword and media research. Without the research and an analysis, it's difficult to prescribe specific strategies.

The second reason is we have not talked yet about which tools are available and should be considered. We'll do that in Chapter 4. there are so many tools from which to choose. Until we cover the web technologies you'll want to use, it is difficult for you to design processes.

Don't begin with too few tools. Abraham Maslow said, "If you only have a hammer, you tend to see every problem as a nail." For example, if you only know about how websites function, but not social media, you'll tend to under-utilize social media. However, Google's biggest competitor right now is not Yahoo or Bing ... it's Facebook. Learn about existing technologies. Later you can come back to design your additional strategies. Let's start with how the Web works in general ... principles that will be valid for most strategies.

HOW THE WEB WORKS

In the early 1990's Michael Dell (Dell Computers) gave a speech at the Detroit Economic Club. He indicated there are three things needed for effective leadership in an online business. They are referred to as The Three C's: Content, Commerce, and Community.

The first of The Three C's is content is your innovations or the ideas you put into a consumable form. Content may be images, photos, written be an-books, podcasts, music, software, video files, webinar content or training programs. There are typically three ways that your followers would find your content:

1. Organic searches ... You type a few keywords into a search engine like Google, Yahoo, or Bing and get a list of websites with the content that matches your keywords. To be found in organic searches you need to rank high. That means being as near the top of the first page of the search results as possible. There are specific steps you can take to get ranked. The process of taking those steps is call search engine optimization or SEO. Companies often hire a specialist to help them with their SEO. We'll look at SEO a little later.

2. Social media ... People may find your content through suggestions made by friends and others they interact with on the Web. This typically takes place in websites and systems that are designed to facilitate these interactions. Social media would include online blogs, forums, Twitter, Facebook, and even YouTube. It includes any system that allows you to comment on content, rate it, or recommend it to others.

3. Driven traffic ... content that is delivered through email campaigns, e-newsletters, RSS feeds, or other means that a consumer has requested. I personally use Google Alerts to find out about new content that is of interest to me. Google notifies you by email when something new has been put on the Web that contains specified search terms. I recommend that you set up Google Alerts for your name and your business name to keep tabs on your reputation on the Web.

The second of The Three C's is commerce. It doesn't necessarily mean commerce in a financial sense like a shopping cart; it refers to your systems for connecting your content and your parade. Your commerce is your website or other webpages you develop. It might include automated email systems, podcast feeds, and text messaging systems, or webcast systems such as Go to Webinar. Social media sites like Facebook and YouTube are certainly commerce systems for delivery of content and creation of community.

The third of The Three C's is community. This has never been more important than it is today. This is how you and your followers can interact with each other. The community systems on the Web are often referred to as social media. They often contain content, but their main purpose is to create the digital equivalent of word-of-mouth promotion and create a place for you to interact synchronously (real time) or asynchronously (not real time). While social sites like Facebook and Google Plus are commerce systems in our definition, their main function is to create community.

I suggest you plan your web strategies around The 3 C's. They make a great framework for the overall design. Using them will keep you from spending all your time in one area to the neglect of the other two. A design curriculum professionally and I often look at The 3 C's to inform my design projects. When you balance the three it keeps your information delivery, relevant, efficient, and enjoyable.

DESIGN FOR SEARCH ENGINE OPTIMIZATION (SEO)

SEO strategies are designed to help your website get ranked and found in search engines. The ideal position is at the top of the first page of Google. That doesn't just happen. Its ranking is based on complex formulas (algorithms) used by Google. These algorithms take into account the name of the website, the keywords in the name and content, the age of the website, the number of visitors, the freshness of the website, and its backlinks.

Backlinks are when another website links to your website. From the beginning of your initiative you want your content and website designed for SEO. A website that has keywords in its domain name will do better in the algorithms than a clever name without keywords. For example, www.puppytraining.com would probably be a better choice than www.youngdognewtricks.com. While *young dog new tricks* may be more creative than *puppy training*, it is probably not what people are typing in when they search.

Other SEO strategies include use of keywords and tags in your web page titles, descriptions, image names, and content, and creating backlinks. Another way is to create backlinks by posting in blogs on your topic which will allow you to include your website address as part of a post. Post relevant information in the blogs. Don't post junk, just to get a backlink. Make it a win-win for you and the blogger. Use keywords in your posts.

Organize your design by using three columns or pages. Label each one each with Content, Commerce, and Community. Look at your elevator speech and then select 3-6 items to put in each column. Prioritize them and then you're ready to start on the development stage. You can always adjust your design as you develop; that is what you do in rapid prototyping. The key is to get started quickly once you have identified a quality niche and audience.

DEVELOP

After designing your strategy you'll want to pick up the pace; you'll move into the actual creation of materials and systems. You may want to have components from the development, implementation, and evaluation stages all at the same time. In the field of instructional design it borrows from a method called rapid prototyping. In other words, it's developing The Three C's all at the same time based on more fluid models Where do these models come from? You generate them from your web research. As you performed your niche or keyword research, you should have encountered web pages of existing thought leaders. This gives you an idea of what the audience will expect. Use them as the starting model. Then improve them.

I consistently use one of about three different models for website development. By doing so, I save all kinds of energy and time making decisions about how the website will function and what the user experience will be. Using a model helps me eliminate costly and time-consuming changes to the structure. I can still customize the model for individual needs of clients by changing color and functionality. However, a standard model saves them significant amounts on their website development costs. You can see one of the main models that I use at www.theleadernextdoor.com.

I utilize WordPress (WP) models of websites (See About WordPress in the next chapter). The WP websites allow you to create content directly in the website. It is a real time-saver; you can create it, format it, or edit it on any computer connected to the Internet with the WP built in text editor. This is a hassle-free way to develop your website and content at the same time. Even if you need to hire someone to set it up for you, from then on you can create content and make changes yourself. It's as easy as writing an email in a WP site.

You can test it as you build it because you instantly experience the look and feel of your content in the web environment. Because it is on the Web, you can get feedback and evaluations from others, especially if you have been engaged in online communities and have connected with potential followers who might review it.

For example, while I'm writing this book, I'm building a website with a blog to support it and engaging in forums with internet marketers and networking offline to meet people who could be potential followers.

Some people prefer to establish their Thought Leadership 2.0 with a sequential approach. They want to develop the content, before they set up their web technologies or engage with a community. Sequential development slows down progress as they try to make each part perfect. The result is they often lose their intentionality because it takes so long, or they get discouraged because they have to change content once they do start getting feedback from followers.

With rapid prototyping you are creating content, commerce, and community and are going through the process of development, implementation, and evaluation all at the same time. That is leveraging your time and energy.

If rapid prototyping doesn't fit your personality style, then you can certainly proceed in a more sequential manner. However, you run the risk of getting bored, sidetracked, or discouraged when the process lengthens. There is also the issue lead time needed for the search engines to locate you. If you can start the SEO process at the same time as your other initiatives, you can have an optimized site ready to kick into high gear.

IMPLEMENT

Implement engagement. You don't need any content to implement engagement. Your engagement can be the beginning of your content. If you have done the research suggested earlier you have probably located some forums or blogs where you can participate in online discussion related to your topic. Doing a search for Facebook Groups is a good place to start. What I like about Facebook groups is they let you know how many members are engaged in each group so you don't waste time with groups that are too small..

Engage in blogs, forums, and groups as you would in a natural conversation. Find discussions where you can respond positively to what's being said. Stay away from the negative conversations. You don't need the hyper-critical or whiners as your followers. Use give and take in your postings. Going in and simply making announcements about your business or products is a turn off. Talk about your ideas when the conversation naturally leads to them or in a way that asks for opinions. People need to like you, trust you, and respect you, before they will follow you. You have to earn that. Remember the definition of leadership says leaders influence others to achieve a common goal. Respond to others twice as much as you promote your own agenda.

If you want to establish a relationship with potential followers, I suggest you use your own name; followers want to follow a real person not "SeattleSam." If you want to use a clever name in your title for branding purposes, then sign the post with your real name. You can't be a thought leader and be anonymous. If it is a forum or blog where you must register to engage, then fill out your profile in a way that represents you well. Include an image of yourself that is professional. It should be friendly and casual enough to encourage friendship but avoid pictures that make you look silly. Keep the picture and information appropriate to your profession or topic. Remember they both become part of your web reputation.

Implement content. You don't have to have huge amounts of content to get started. I wouldn't go to the store and buy enough fresh lettuce for a year... I buy small amounts often. Consistent development to produce fresh content and interactions with community is more important than huge quantities all at once. The most important thing is to get started quickly and be consistent. You want to know as soon as possible what the viability of your niche is. With the tools available today, getting started is not an issue. Ideally, start with simple content you can develop and implement within two to four weeks.

After you have the beginning content and systems, I suggest you add a personal blog to your website. Your interaction in other blogs and forums should provide you with an idea of the needs and questions your potential followers have. In your blog, start addressing those issues. A simple blog post of 50 to 75 words that answers a relevant question is a good way to get started. It's better to write a short post a couple of times a week, than to do one large post once in a while.

If you are addressing something that needs more detail than 100 words or so, I suggest writing 500-600 words and produce it as an article rather than a blog post. You can publish the article on the Web with a link back to your blog, and then link to the article in a blog post if readers want more information. This strategy generates mutual backlinks. Include your keywords in your blog posts as frequently as possible but not so much that your writing becomes odd.

EVALUATE

If you limit yourself to what you can create and implement in less than four weeks, you implement quickly so you can move on to test your content and delivery. You'll want to evaluate what you've done. You can't do that without exposing your content to followers for feedback. If you've engaged several potential followers online you should now try to engage them in your website, especially your blog. Continue to engage in the other places as you have been, but to turn them into followers, engage them on your site with your content. You want to save your best content for delivery on your website. The best evaluation is requesting feedback from them regarding your site and your content.

Another good evaluation technique is to email friends and colleagues who are somewhat familiar with your topic. Ask them to evaluate your content for clarity, uniqueness, and any other criteria. Ask them to evaluate your website to make sure it is easy to navigate and has an easy-to-understand structure. Keep your evaluation simple and quick. There comes a point of diminishing returns where further evaluation yields less worthwhile results.

ADJUST AND LEVERAGE

From your feedback select two or three changes, adjust your content and systems by implementing them and evaluate again. It is the principle of CANI (Constant and Never-ending Improvement) that Dr. Edward Deming brought to Japan after World War II. It transformed Japanese manufacturing. Deming taught Japanese managers that constant and small improvements, continued over time, were more productive than huge jumps of sporadic improvement. That is the model of rapid prototyping: designing, developing, evaluating and adjustments all going on simultaneously or in very short time frames. You just keep rotating that pattern.

Another adjustment you need to make is to the content you create. There are two ways that are suggested to grow a business and they apply to the development of Thought Leadership 2.0. One is to take a new product into an existing market. The other is to take an existing product into a new market.

Both of these are less risky than taking a new product into a new market. When you begin to take your ideas into existing forums, you are taking a new product into an existing market. You then bring members of that market to your website to consume your content. You'll want to keep them interested by developing new content.

You can adjust your existing content into new formats to expand the number of followers you can reach; in other words, take it into new markets. For example, you can write articles to publish and link to in your blog. You might plan the articles to be a part of a bigger entity. You then combine those articles into a book that is self-published through Amazon or Barnes and Noble. Publishing it starts reaching a new market. Additionally, authoring a book is a powerful way of positioning yourself as a 2.0 thought leader.

Let's reverse engineer the process. If you have a book, you can take excerpts from it to use as blog posts. Taking the outline of an article, you can turn it into a video to post in YouTube or other such websites. You can create a backlink in YouTube from your video back to your website. There are many ways for you to reuse or repurpose your content and to leverage existing content into a new market.

Another adjustment you should consider is leveraging your community. Including "Like" buttons on your site encourages your followers to recommend your site to others. Using Facebook you might create a Fan Page and when your followers click on the "Like" button, it is posted on their friends' Facebook pages. Another method of this kind of leverage would be to put links to your blog, articles, or videos in Twitter Tweets. Encourage your followers to follow you on Twitter and ask them to re-tweet your messages to their followers. That's leveraging the power of community with web technologies.

Don't be overwhelmed by what you've read. You don't have to do everything at once. You don't have to understand it all. You'll learn it piece by piece. There are lots of ways to outsource some of the work, especially the commerce side of it.

The important thing is to get started where you can. You can adjust and improve as you go along. Remember the development of The Three C's is a journey not a destination. The Three C's have guided Dell Computers to success. There is a Development Planner Worksheet available for you at www.theleadernextdoor.com.

CHAPTER 4

CORE TECHNOLOGIES

"Want to strengthen your thought leadership?

Crown yourself and assume the throne.

Use opinion, story, credentials to build authority."

- Andrea J. Lee

You have to use some core technologies to build your authority. This may mean you need to learn some new technologies. Even if you don't want to be a technologist and intend to outsource the technology work, you should learn enough to understand the process. Learning a little about how technologies work will not only put you in a position to better manage your outsourcing, but it will increase your ability to create and solve problems utilizing those technologies. I'm going to assume you've already done your keyword research and know your niche. I'm going to share with you some of the popular technologies in use. They are not the only ones available; I simply like the way they have worked for me.

TECHNOLOGIES TO CONSIDER

I will give a brief commentary on several different technologies to help you with your research and decision-making. They are not intended to be how-to manuals. If you need training or want more information, browser searches and YouTube searches will provide you with lots of training. I often start my search with "How to." It's rare when someone else hasn't had the same questions. I have links to some training on the technologies available under *Thought Leadership Resources* at www.theleadernextdoor.com.

GMAIL

I always start with a Gmail account for each niche. I try to get a separate Gmail for separate topics which have the keywords in the name or share the name of your main website for that topic. For example, if your niche is new cell phone apps and the domain name www.newcellphoneapps.com is available, then I would try to get newcellphoneapps@gmail.com as my email to use for the topic. Typically, I do a preliminary name search to find the domain name I want and then try to get the counterpart as my Gmail account. Names with locations are often helpful for local businesses. For example, a golf pro who wants to establish herself but works in a local area might choose a name that is reflective of the area where the business operates such as www.tampagolflessons.com. While the name may not be extremely clever, people in Tampa who are looking for a golf pro are more likely to find it since search engines often determine the geographic location of the computer and prioritize selections based upon it. They really try to give you relevant material. While you're setting up you Gmail account, it is a good time to set up Google Alerts for your name and your business name.

DOMAINSITE

When I have the Gmail account I want, I use it as the contact email for setting up all accounts related to that topic. I usually purchase my domain names through www.domainsite.com, but there are many other sites where you can purchase them.

HOST GATOR

Once the Gmail and domain name are purchased you need web hosting. I like www.hostgator.com. They have great customer service by chat or phone. They do weekly back-ups. Their prices are reasonable. Sometimes one website is not enough. Sometimes a second or third website is needed for a specific purpose. (You may want a general website; you may want a lead capture site, and you may need another site to integrate with a Facebook page.) Several simple sites with a single purpose or target audience in mind may be more useful and less confusing to your audience than one large site containing everything but the kitchen sink.

I have a client, Dr. Lourdes Ferrer, who had a website for several years which used her name, www.drlourdes.net. She recently published a book on the subject of Hispanic parental involvement. Google searches for *Hispanic parental involvement* produced first page results for videos and articles I produced for her, but not her website. Finally, we decided to create another, website to promote her new book. We named it: www.hispanicparentalinvolvement.com. It had the keywords in the domain name. It ranked on the first page of Google within a week. Her initial website still is her brand: The second one is used for a specific targeted message. We come to another point. Some of Host Gator's accounts allow you to host more than one domain on the same account. It saves you money over setting up individual accounts.

One of the things I like about a Host Gator account is the Cpanel feature which is an administrative interface for the account. Once Cpanel feature is that you can set up an email forwarder which will forward yourname@yourwebsite.com to your Gmail or any other account. Another feature is the *Fantastico* technology. Fantastico will automate the installation of selected technologies into your website. I create many WP websites. WordPress is one of the options with Fantastico. It makes it simple to create a WP website.

WORDPRESS

There is a learning curve to WordPress but it is definitely worth the time it takes. Even if you decide to hire someone to develop your website for you, it is a good idea to request for them to develop it with WordPress. WordPress allows you the anytime, anywhere editing without other programs. Furthermore, it can be customized with mini add-on programming features called plugins. The WordPress organization has hundreds of plugins. There are plugins for shopping carts, ordering the pages, membership, and changing numerous other features in WordPress. Once you have a domain name and web hosting, WordPress is free software. While it is possible to set up a WordPress blog hosted by WordPress, you don't get some benefits which come from hosting it yourself with your own domain name. When installed, WordPress can be a very functional site. If you decide to use a blog as one of the features, remember that a blog is a commitment. You need to blog on a regular basis or not at all.

YOUTUBE

Video marketing is one of the most powerful engines for reaching people with your message. YouTube is now the third most visited website in the world. According to Alexa.com, it gets more than 300 million visitors per month who watch more than 2 billion videos. Video marketing is turbo-charged. Marketing on YouTube is one of the fastest ways to get found by Google. Video marketing is part of an effective strategy to establish yourself as a thought-leader in your field and gain the kind of web following which will result in more followers. People go there to look for videos to answer their questions, solve their problems, and provide information about products and businesses. When you create your account, you can create your own YouTube channel. There are ways to put backlinks in your YouTube videos to your website. YouTube is technology worth learning and using.

MORE ABOUT TECHNOLOGY FOR VIDEO

Video for the Web can be as simple as a PowerPoint presentation with narration. It works for creating video to distribute through sharing sites like YouTube, Vimeo, and others. I recommend you start with PowerPoint converted to video until you have tested your topic and niche. If the whole process of video or audio production seems intimidating, then I suggest you take time to experiment with it. There is a lot you can do with the other tools mentioned above. However, with today's technology, video using PowerPoint isn't out of reach.

If you have PowerPoint 2010, you can record a narration using PowerPoint tools or narrate it with using files exported from Audacity. The easiest way is to create a separate sound file for each slide. In PowerPoint 2010 you can rehearse the timings and then use the Save and Send feature to convert it to a video. Many computers come with programs like Movie Maker which can be used by exporting your PowerPoint presentation as a series of slides and then adding narration in the movie making software and producing it.

My favorite program for recording video is Camtasia which will record a PowerPoint presentation while you play it. It is not a free program but you can download a 30-day trial. It has excellent training on its website. Camtasia allows you to produce the finished product in multiple video formats. I typically use MP4 to upload to YouTube. Camtasia is available at www.techsmith.com.

An alternative to Camtasia is iSpring Free which is available from www.ispringsolutions.com. It produces the presentation as a Flash video you can upload to your YouTube channel. Both Camtasia and iSpring reside as add-ons for PowerPoint. As an add-on they are on the ribbon at the top of PowerPoint and you click on them to use them without opening them as a separate program. Depending on your skill level in technology, video production may or may not sound difficult to you. If video is a bit overwhelming, then concentrate on using other tools.

FACEBOOK

To be active where your target is, you need to spend some time on Facebook. There are more than 400 million Facebook users and 50% of them log on to Facebook on any given day, mostly from home or school. It is the number two visited website in the world (Alexa.com). according to Alexa.com. There are 1.5 million local businesses with active Pages on Facebook. They use them to establish their reputation and create relationships. More than 20 million people become fans of Pages each day. A Facebook strategy should start with a profile that promotes your expertise without being pushy. Then a Fan Page should be created to serve your topic. You may need to educate yourself on how to create a Fan Page. A YouTube search will provide you with the training you need. Earlier we talked about Facebook Groups. Once you get some followers on your Fan Page, you may want to form your own Facebook Group around your topic.

LINKEDIN

What Facebook is to social networking, Linkedin is to business networking. It is the 11th ranked website in the U.S. by Alexa.com. There are a higher percentage of people with graduate degrees accessing Linkedin than with Facebook. Another interesting difference is that while people tend to access Facebook at home or school, a higher percentage access Linkedin from work. I'm not suggesting that you use Linkedin instead of Facebook but rather, in addition to it. Facebook is too big to ignore. If you are looking for a social media tool that may be a good source of professional contacts, you may want to visit www.linkedin.com and set up an account.

TWITTER

Alexa.com ranks Twitter as ninth in website popularity. It is called micro-blogging because of the limited characters you can post at one time in a message. It's very much like text messaging. Like Linkedin, Twitter has a higher educated user group than Facebook and tends to be accessed at school or work in a larger way. If you're going to use Twitter to link to a website, you need to shorten the web addresses using a service such as www.tinyurl.com There's lots of training material on the Web on how to set up accounts and utilize Twitter. A word of caution: don't send Tweets (Twitter messages) about trivial information. "Got up - Had Coffee" is not a Tweet to enhance your Thought Leadership 2.0. As with all good web marketing, it's not about you; it's about what your followers need. You can set up your account at www.twitter.com. Try to set up a name that is easy to remember and type, and which is related to your website. Your Twitter account will be accessed as www.twitter.com/yourname.

SCRIBD

Scribd claims to be: "the world's largest social reading and publishing company." Scribd is a document sharing site used by Ford Motor Company, CBS, Fox News, Simon and Shuster, and you. You can use it to publish articles in various formats as an article marketing strategy. Millions of articles have been published on Scribd. As part of the publishing process you can create a backlink to your website. I've published several articles and have over 43,000 views. You want to make sure the title and content of the articles are keyword rich. Doing so, I've had Scribd articles make the first page of Google in a selected niche. You can set up an account at www.scribd.com. This is a good place to start article marketing. One of best features of Scribd is it provides you with statistics about each article's viewership.

SLIDESHARE

Slide Share is also a document sharing site, but its strength is presentations, PDFs, and webinars. In fact it boasts of being the world's largest presentation sharing website with nearly 50 million monthly visitors viewing 90 million pages. It is used by entities like Pfizer, Dell, the White House, the Army and Navy, and a number of universities. It is among the top 250 most visited websites in the world. It was recently voted in the top 10 tools for education and learning. It is well worth setting up an account. As a strategy, I suggest you publish an article on Scribd and then re-purpose it as a PowerPoint to publish on Slide Share. I like to put the website address as a hyperlink in my PowerPoint. When uploaded the hyperlink creates a backlink and is a way for new followers to get to the main website. Go to www.slideshare.net.

AMAZON

Amazon is rated number 15 of the top websites by Alexa.com. As a 2.0 thought leader, selling your information on Amazon helps you get found. If you are careful how you do it, you can even get a backlink to your website in your description or bio. Publishing a book which is sold on Amazon is not as difficult as jumping through the hoops to get an independent publisher to do it. Amazon has a division at www.createspace.com that will help you through the process. They provide you with an ISBN number and tools to format a book. You can publish it in both printed and Kindle versions. For a nominal fee they will put your book in a system which distributes it not only to Amazon, but also to Barnes and Noble and others.

You do not have to buy hundreds of dollars of books to get started. They utilize print-on-demand so the books are not printed until they are sold. They will print paperback books with 24 pages or more and will print smaller content on Kindle. This is an excellent strategy for establishing yourself as a 2.0 thought leader.

AUDACITY

An additional software you may need is Audacity. Audacity is free software for recording and editing sound files. You can create audio files for narrating PowerPoint presentations which can in turn, be turned into videos for uploading to YouTube. You can use Audacity for creating podcasts and even audio books. It is available from: audacity.sourceforge.net. When you record in Audacity you will want to Export it rather than using the Save feature. Exporting it allows you to save files as a WAV or MP3 files which are more usable formats.

AWEBER

If you want to do an email campaign, you will need a system to handle it for you. You may want to look at Aweber. Over 102,000 businesses use Aweber email software to deliver their marketing campaigns and newsletters. Aweber has tools to help you generate web forms to place in your website. It will auto deliver a message when potential followers fill out the form. You can then use Aweber to periodically deliver other content to your email list. They provide convenient opt-outs so people can automatically stop delivery of emails. This protects you from complaints of spamming. To learn more you can go to www.aweber.com.

This covers some core technologies you will want to consider as you design your web initiatives. You can find most of what you need in training to use them on the Web. I recommend starting with YouTube searches. Now it's time to take action.

CHAPTER 5

START

"We cannot do everything at once, but we can do something at once."

- Calvin Coolidge

If I allow it, I can get bogged down in the paralysis of the analysis. I spend so much time analyzing and thinking creatively around a subject until one of the following occurs:

- I have to "wait until the time is right" to tackle it.

- The project becomes so big and protracted I lose interest

- I get distracted by a newer idea.

The result was half-completed projects. I've wanted to write a book for years but kept switching topics or the process was too daunting to start. Something changed for me. Dr. Lourdes Ferrer hired me to publish her book, *Hispanic Parental Involvement*. It was a lot of work. I helped with the concept, was a content editor, formatted the book, and designed the cover art. It was a milestone when it finally appeared on Amazon and Barnes and Noble. I then helped her with

SEO. If you do a Google search for "Hispanic Parental Involvement," you will easily find her in the niche.

Afterwards I had a time of reflection about how well it worked and realized the power of personal publishing. It led me to develop a specific process.

ROTATING THE PATTERN

Years ago I was in a part-time business where Bill Lewis, one of its leaders, taught a process of rotating a pattern to achieve success. It's one of the principles which is the basis of franchising. You develop a pattern (a system) and then repeat the pattern over and over, rotating through the sequential steps. I decided to apply that to niche writing and materials development. I decided to develop a pattern.

I decided the pattern was going to be writing 40 - 80 page mini-books that provided the best information I had on topics about which I was knowledgeable and passionate. (Does it sound like GPA?) I wanted to write books that I could finish in eight weeks or less.

These would be books that the reader could consume in a night or two of reading. In today's environment many people want you to be brief, say something significant, and then be done with it. After writing the book I could continue with the other web promotion activities we've covered earlier. These would include articles, videos, and other related media. Then I would rotate the pattern and start another book. Thought Leadership 2.0 is the first book in the pattern. I developed a seven-step pattern:

1. Set-up: Create an outline for the book based upon keyword research.

2. Write a 40-80 page book while setting up the commerce side of things at the same time.

3. Publish and promote the book.

4. Re-purpose some of the book content into articles, presentations, and videos for SEO.

5. Find and engage followers.

6. Develop a webinar around the niche.

7. Monetize the system by marketing training around the niche.

I have ten titles or topics ready chose from for the start of the next rotation. This pattern will allow me to avoid being overly invested in any one book because there is another one waiting to be written. If one book fails, it happens quickly and there is another one ready to take its place. Note that step three of my pattern is a loop within the pattern. Once a book is finished I will loop back to begin writing on another while continuing through the rotation with the first book.

START!

I share my story with you to encourage you. Start somewhere. Keep it simple but start it with a plan to build momentum. Start with something you can accomplish in a month or two and go on from there. In *Rework*, Jason Fried and David Heinemeier Hansson state, "Momentum fuels motivation. It keeps you going. It drives you. Without it, you can't go anywhere." They continue, "The way you build momentum is by getting something done and then moving on to the next thing."

That is what I hope you will do. Start with the steps you can. Build one piece of content. Start one commerce system. Find one community member. Build your momentum from there.

I leave you with this thought from Vance Havner: "The vision must be followed by the venture. It is not enough to stare up the steps - we must step up the stairs." Take your first step. Let your light shine.

RESOURCES

Many of the resources
mentioned in this book are available at
http://www.theleadernextdoor.com

If you are interested in consulting
you may contact Rick Hubbard
at the above website.

Much of the training needed
for the technologies described here
may be found by basic web searches in
Google, YouTube, and other search engines.

Rick Hubbard

www.ingramcontent.com/pod-product-compliance
Lightning Source LLC
Chambersburg PA
CBHW051244170526
45165CB00004B/1575